INTERIORS IN COLOR

INTERIORS IN COLOR

INTERIORS IN COLOR

Creating Space, Personality and Atmosphere

By Mirko Mejetta and Simonetta Spada
Translated by Anthony de Alteriis, AIA

Whitney Library of Design
An imprint sof Watson-Guptill Publications, New York

First published in the United States and Canada
by the Whitney Library of Design,
an imprint of Watson-Guptill Publications,
1515 Broadway, New York, N.Y. 10036

Library of Congress Cataloging in Publication Data

Mejetta, Mirko
Interiors in color.

1. Color in interior decoration. I. Spada, Simonetta.
II. Title.
NK2115.5. C6M44   1983   747'.94   83-3446
ISBN 0-8230-7301-7

Copyright © Gruppo Editoriale Electa, Milan 1983

Translation copyright © by Whitney Library of Design

Printed by Fantonigrafica, Venice/Italy, a company of
Gruppo Editoriale Electa
First printing 1983

CONTENTS

Managing Editor
Dorothea Balluff

Texts
Mirko Mejetta

Art direction/Layout
Simonetta Spada

Photos by:
Brigitte Baert (p. 20)
Mariarosa Ballo (p. 91)
Anka and Reiner Blunck (p. 56)
Claus Bonderup (p. 46)
Brecht-Einzig (p. 22)
Enrico Calvani (p. 19)
Fabio Cianchetti (p. 26)
Carla De Benedetti (p. 14)
Gilles De Chabanneix (pp. 30, 81)
Antonia Giacometti (p. 10)
Alessandro Gui (p. 76)
Pierrik Maze' (p. 48)
Maria Mulas (p. 86)
Grazia Neri (p. 48)
J. Primois (p. 20)
Enzo Pucciarelli (p. 19)
Francis Rambert (p. 80)
Marvin Rand (p. 60)
Bent Rey (p. 40)
Laura Salvati (pp. 42, 64, 94, and cover)
Bob Sasson (p. 80)
Roberto Sellitto (p. 36)
Tim Street Porter/EWA (p. 72)
Stefano Valabrega (pp. 68, 77)
Fabio Zonta (p. 53)
Giuliana Zoppis (p. 26)

To furnish and decorate one's own home with furniture and other objects, and to paint these as well as the walls, doors and windows, is both a private act and an act of communication. The way one lives at home is a language one uses to express one's feelings, convey memories and nostalgia, and visibly state one's longings. Even if the house of the future should prove to be a bare basic dwelling infinitely repeated, we will continue to fill it with objects which express our personality, our own chosen colors; we will continue to make it into a personal thing, tailored to our own selves and to our emotions, ahead of our functional needs.

To think of the home as a container which answers only basic needs is unrealistic, just as it is unrealistic to plan a house as something untouchable, something which never changes. The blue door of a house makes us think of large internal spaces, luminous and calm; the chair, of a warm yellow, seems soft and almost clinging. Color takes on the quality of evoking feelings, letting us travel swiftly through feeling and memories. Architecture which is not authoritarian, which can be lived in, must be able to accept additions, changes, any number of objects and embellishments—in sum, the many levels of the highly personal and private lifestyle of the residents.

Color, its many uses, combinations and relationships, its metaphors and symbols, belongs, when furnishing a house, to the realm of expression, of feeling, of awareness of one's self. The reds, yellows and blues are perceived more quickly than shapes or sounds, and are the best way of transmitting sensations and information in our society.

The many scientific theories of color tend to impose a strict and absolute system over something which is in fact relative for different cultures, intimate, not measurable. Color is the artificial means which mankind has from the beginning used to imitate the reality of nature, picturing it; then interpreting it; and finally abandoning it in favor of building a human reality. Color is imagination, creativity, an intellectual and literary instrument.

This book is not a do-it-yourself manual, but a collection of impressions, carefully selected and arranged, aimed at stimulating the reader to reflect on the use of color in the furnishing of his or her own house — not by imitation, but freely and spontaneously.

COLOR AS DECORATION

Traditional San Francisco architecture, decorated in delicate pastel colors

PATTERNS IN COLOR

Color, modest and delicate, draws in on itself so as not to oppress and overwhelm the calm architecture of the 1800's. This fascinating structure of glass and cast iron belongs to an aristocratic villa in the Venetian hinterland. The designer, Pino Danieli, has transformed the long, narrow gallery of the old greenhouse into a brightly lit room for a young fashion designer.

The furniture runs along the walls, tightening the rhythm of the vertical window frames, the glass panes, and the cast iron columns. All the furniture, designed by the artist Mario Ceroli, is in natural wood. The settees, covered with flat cushions in white or pastel tints, recall by their shape the curvilinear design of the iron structure, their thin, vertical lamelle marking a continuous, repetitive movement interrupted or halted only by the unifying presence of the large points of color: the telescopic totem by Ettore Sottsass, and the feminine figure in decorated wood by Rod Dudley, accompanied by the agile and slender shape of the wooden greyhound.

On the vault the colored decorations cut sharply into the space: the graffiti by the painter Licata hold your eye, a kind of magical and mysterious background, a vital complement to the rarified, theatrical atmosphere of the

(Large photograph): the long perspective view of the greenhouse-living room, with settees and tables in natural wood designed by artist Mario Ceroli; in the background, the colored totem is by Ettore Sottsass and the feminine figure by Rod Dudley.

(Small photograph): the two wooden sculptures by Rod Dudley stand out against the background of the great park of the Venetian villa in springtime.

overall space. The strongly woven design of outlines and opaque color lightens the mass of the wall, recreating the effect of transparency and openness of the long glass wall. On the other half of the vault, the light which filters through curtains of blue stripes placed in front of the glass gives an even greater dynamic quality to the structure, intensifying its depth of perspective.

From the floor of soft rose Verona marble, slender pilasters of cast iron stretch upward, decorated with palmettos and interlaced flowers, and contrasting with the simple geometry of the iron bases along the periphery. In this scheme, color and decoration are almost synonomous.

In the paving of St. Mark's Cathedral, we find the best example of the use of color as pattern. The delicate triangles of colored stones make the floor a definite, unique object, with shape and thickness: a three-dimensional composition, not a simple plane surface.

Color, then, acquires three-dimensional body when it is used as a geometrical abstraction, as an artificial and evocative graffito. Color as pattern comes into the design and manufacture of furniture and furnishings not only as a decorative element but also, above all, as an expressive way of uniting decoration, form and structure.

(From the top): glass walls and vault of the old greenhouse. Exterior view of the 19th century villa. The dining room adjoining the greenhouse: chairs and table in solid wood are by Ceroli, the sculpture of birds is by Codognotto and Abadan.

(On this page):
Top: colored graffiti, in green, azure, violet, and orange, decorate a row of ceramic tile.
Middle: detail of the floor of the Basilica of St. Mark in Venice.
Bottom right: a Me-la chair, carried out in an unusual graphical form in epoxy painted metal tubing and plywood of various colors.
Bottom left: four examples of ceramic tile, colored and decorated using spot, dribble, and crater techniques.

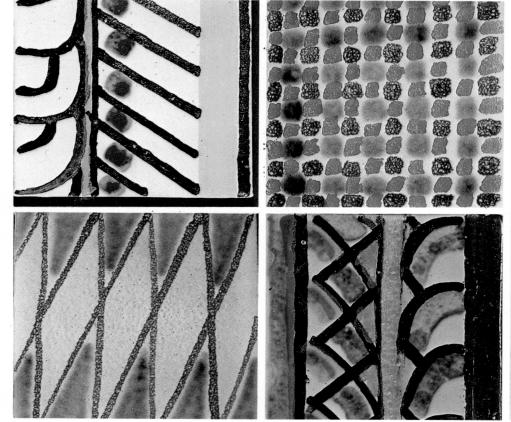

COLOR DIFFUSED

The New York loft decorated by Louis Meisel resembles the kind of giant toy box into which children drop all their toys in a big jumble. On raising the lid, a windstorm of colors comes rushing out, so that you cannot separate red from blue, turquoise from straw. The colors are everywhere, superimposed on each other, spreading themselves uniformly throughout the space.
In this loft, the kitchen and dining table, library and sleeping area, are placed side by side, in open plan and open to view. The furnishings, heaped up and overflowing, give color to the space as they would in a large shop, following each other about from kitchen counter to the nooks above the bed, from the book shelves to the wall behind the table: furnishings recognizable more by their color than by their shape. While the strong iron columns, the beams and pipes which span the room are treated without emphasis and painted white, thus reduced to a silent, anonymous background, the large realistic pictures on the walls epitomize, movingly and expressively, the feeling of this house. Here, a love for banal household articles (a vase, a bowl) and for street furniture (signs, penny chewing-gum machines) is tied to a pleasure in the play of color and to a variety of shape which is almost child-like. The grouping of subtle stripes and spots of color on the earthen bowls above the studio couch is like a puzzle, in which all the pieces resemble each other and mingle, with only the undecipherable spots of color allowing one to distinguish one from the other.

The large kitchen counter with snack bar-type stools is backed by generous open shelves. To the right, the refrigerator in metal and glass is of the type used in supermarkets. The big store-type scale is white, with bronze decoration. The whole space is lighted by small spot lights hung from tracks.

The soft green of the shelves and of the patterned tiles above the kitchen sink just about manage to impose order on the colors, which range from the long band of red Campbell's soup cans to the golden decoration of the old weighing scales, from the warm tan of cookies in a jar to the bright colors of fruit in a soup bowl, from the neat row of white cups to the electric mixture of bottles and packages behind the glass front of the high-tech refrigerator. In this interior, color is everywhere, given over more to abundance than to individual strength. It envelops the space, weaving among the different areas of the house, thus increasing one's perception of an open, unified space.

(Right):
overall view of the loft. To the left is the large kitchen space and to the right the dining area and its ample, metal book shelving. The different spaces are related to each other to make one big space ready to welcome large numbers of people.

(Right):
the bed, which also serves as a couch, flanks a wall with built-in shelves for the multi-colored earthenware. On the wall a large grazing cow looks out, calm and restful.

(Left):
the dining area as seen from the kitchen counter. The large wood-topped table is surrounded by folding chairs of wood and fabric. The wall is reserved for large, realistic paintings visible from all over the loft. Large scale dishes of asparagus, jars of chewing gum, the shining, roaring metal of a Formula 1 car, color and warm the space with their cheer.

COLORED SURFACES

Tiger-striped or spongy, criss-crossed or dotted – the new surfaces slip into the house, putting a new dress on walls and floors, furniture and furnishings. The walls of rooms revolve first about themselves; then, kitchen and living room, bed and studio impulsively join to make one, large space. The house renounces complex volumes, the play of solid and void; furnishings and furniture are subdued in shadow. It is the light, the color and the pattern of surfaces that dominate the space of the house.

The picture we get is of a sensation, an "ambiance."

Classical theories on the use of color in interiors speak of the size effect and the temperature of colors: white enlarges space, black decreases it; red warms and blue cools. In addition, however, each of us forms personal relationships between color and feeling, physical sensations, memories. The world of color rules, but only in terms of one's own cultural background, personality and memories.

On riverbanks, spontaneous architectural creations rise swiftly and disappear, shelters for weekend fishermen. Isolated, unseen even by the occasional stroller, the fantastic surfaces of these huts by a river reveal a love for shape and color which remains silent and hidden in our houses; they speak of harmonic and chromatic relationships, spontaneous and free.

Plastic laminate is a material made of a paper base sheet impregnated with phenolic resin, and protected by a decorative sheet impregnated with melamine resin which gives the sheet its color or pattern. Shown is a selection of plastic laminates by well-known designers Ettore Sottsass, Paola Navone, Mario Radice and Andrea Branzi.

Pictures show details of fishermen's huts at the mouth of the Arno River near Pisa. Simple storage places, they have transformed themselves into spontaneously decorated mini-houses. The huts are built from scrap materials: wood, iron, glass, cloth, paper, plastic and vegetable materials.

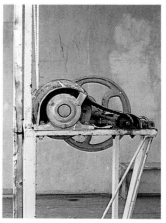

COLORS OF THE SUN

It's an insistent color, reddish, that explodes and spreads. It jumps over the boundary wall, encroaches on the road, and stretches calmly onto the sidewalk; then suddenly it pulls back, sucked in by the black hole of the doorway; it surrounds the house and rises swiftly, a delicate yellow splash of water and light. A thousand and one are the suns that light up the earth. Every corner of the world has its own colors from its own sun and these enter into people's eyes, their streets, their houses.

Mathias Goeritz live in Cuernavaca, Mexico, in an old villa the artist has gathered about himself like a multi-colored poncho, impudent and joyful. The yellow cube, over 20 feet high and made higher by Goeritz, dominates the red boundary wall and the sidewalk which surround the house. The interior of the villa is arranged around three walls that divide the space into living room, dining room and bedroom. Colored dividing walls help unify the various parts of the house and break up the severity of the interior.

The dining room looks out on the garden through enormous openings of four windows, six feet square. The giant window panes are picked out of the warm ochre walls by thin black frames.

The dividing walls, the square windows and the floor paved in terra cotta become, through their colors, the elements which create this architectural space, open, and penetrated by nature and the garden.

(Top):
facade of the villa with red boundary wall. Wall and sidewalk fix the presence of the villa sharply in the surrounding countryside.

(Bottom):
dining room wall with the four large windows, six feet square, which look out onto the garden. Slender, black frames pick out the glazing from the cruciform, ochre wall.

(Right):
view of the living room inside the yellow cube. The red and yellow dividing walls separate it from the other spaces of the house. The floor is in square terracotta tiles and the doors with the long tubular handles are painted black.

INTRINSIC COLOR

The fascination of natural materials is in the color and warmth of fired material such as brick and tile, and of wood. Floor and ceiling run parallel to each other, taking each other's measure. The Paris home of English architect Richard Rogers, one of the designers of the Beaubourg Center, is a rare example of discipline and simplicity. Simple materials dominate, and the furnishings are essential pieces that bring into relief the windows on the square and the deep feeling of perspective of the space. Reconstruction has removed existing structural members which had created two distinct levels in the large fourteen foot high space, baring the original structure with its load bearing beams. The large, new space is resolved into one volume, in which an attic space above forms the sleeping quarters for the parents while below are the children's room and toilet facilities, screened off from the one space that is living room, dining room and kitchen. The food preparation area is an island with cooking range and sink set into a heat resistant laminated work surface. Beyond the kitchen there is another

(Above):
the grand Place des Vosges, Paris, where Victor Hugo lived and where the beautiful Countess of Castiglione spent time in voluntary isolation to hide from the world her first wrinkles. Today, Richard Rogers, one of the designers of the Beaubourg Center, lives in a house reconstructed by him, a rare example of discipline and simplicity.

(Right):
the spacious room was worked out as one volume in which an attic contains the bedrooms. The kitchen counter is in white plastic laminate with range and sinks built in.

bedroom, which can be closed off by a thick sliding partition, but which becomes part of the main space during the day.

Clay fired materials and wood, when used for what they are, in a single minded and frankly functional way, are able to suspend a place in time, to abstract it from the present. This house would therefore seem so suspended, were it not for the outpouring of splashes of yellow roll shades and of soft couches, as well as other materials crude in contrast — the stainless steel and leather of the chairs and armchairs. Here, the vivid color is secondary, impudent but marginal, in a harmony where the original strength of the materials dominates, underscored by the large areas of white plaster.

The taste of color combinations, clean and controlled, is expressed in this house as in Rogers' other works: walls are white and highlight the roof structure, restored to its original condition, as well as the natural tile floor. The fixed furniture is also white, while chairs and armchairs have a stainless steel frame covered in natural leather, whose color closely matches the color of the tile floor.

The only note of intense color is the yellow of the informal couches and the roll shades.

COLOR AND MATERIAL

The Talbot Street Train is the name of the San Diego, California house, designed and furnished by architect Tom Grondona. The interior of the house seems to be limitless, one room flowing after another in a long chain, as in a game of dominoes. Openings, doorways, high and low level inside windows break down all barriers, always offering glimpses into a new area of the house. One never feels as though one is in only one room, but always in two or three spaces at once. Light, hurtling down through windows, from skylights revealing adjacent spaces, penetrates the rooms, dominates them, changing them into an open air house, luminous and available.

Color allows itself to be dominated by light, adjusting itself so as to accentuate the character of the materials. The brown of the carpet makes the floor even softer and more resilient. The impressive tiled frames of the inside window openings and window sills, the curved line in the dining room become even heavier, shiny and cold in their metallic "taxi yellow." While the plexiglass skylight diffuses a calm blue-green light, the fire engine red makes the iron pilaster of the corner window even stronger and friendlier.

At Talbot Street, color becomes dependent on the materials, enriching and reinforcing their innate qualities.

(Top):
the living room with the modular couch flanked by two walls. On the brown carpet, the spaghetti-like sculpture is called "Your Basic Italian Landscape."

(Bottom):
main facade of Tom Grondona's house, surrounded by the green of San Diego, California. The sinuous line of the house is highlighted by window frames of a different color on each facade of the house. In the background, the blue plexiglass cupola admits light to the dining room. Two views of the dining area, with a blue cupola skylight above. At left the snack bar is finished with strong yellow tiles. The color gets to depend on the material, highlighting and enriching it.

By contrast, the purism of Rietveld, Van Doesburg and Mondrian, and the lively dynamism of the Russian constructivists bring to mind designs which glorify the symbolic status of colors, their capacity to superimpose themselves upon materials, compressing them, even neutralizing them. Rietveld's Red and Blue chair, designed during World War I, has always set itself out as a manifesto for the decorative purity of color: the primary colors, red, blue and yellow and the black of the frame, strongly express a love for a rational, anti-romantic color language as a medium of human communication. The Red and Blue chair represents a world of pure and immaterial things, "anti-natural" and only perceived intellectually.

(Top):
two views of the bathroom with walls and shelf tops finished in yellow tile which identifies all the toilet/kitchen area of the house. At left, the framed door opening joins bath to bedroom. Separation of the spaces is by means of a reddish-purple roll shade.

(Right):
the dining area is visually united with the kitchen by an opening. Through the window on the right, the far wing of the house may be seen as it winds like a train along the length of the site. The entire house is 80 feet long and only 18 to 27 feet wide.

Perhaps only the creative ability and technical knowledge of Charles Eames, through his curves of wood and leather, his iron and steel lines, have succeeded in reaching the limits of purist poetry, rediscovering the demands and innate qualities of materials.

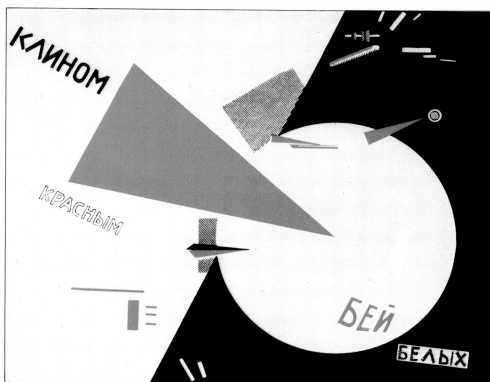

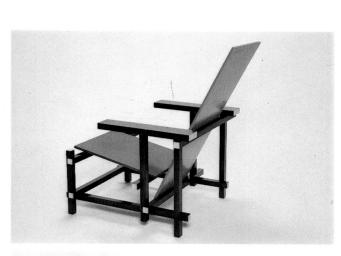

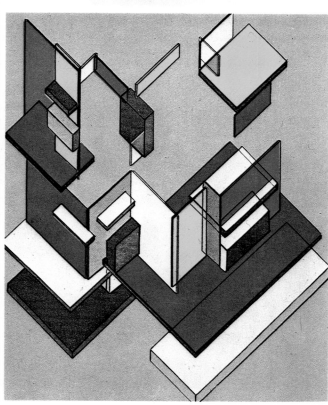

(Left, top to bottom): the Red and Blue chair by Gerrit Rietveld, the image of a world of pure and immaterial things, anti-nature and only perceivable intellectually.

(Center): three chairs of recent Italian manufacture demonstrate the tendency to focus color ever more sharply.

(Bottom) armchair from the "Aluminum Group" by Charles Eames, designer in basic materials.

(On right, from top to bottom): the constructivist manifesto of El Lissitzky "Strike the white with red wedge" (1919).

(Middle): also by Rietveld, a table designed for the 1924 Schroder house in Utrecht.

(Bottom): a neoplastic study based on dematerialization of surfaces through the use of color, by Theo Van Doesburg and Cor Van Eesteren (1920).

THE COLORS OF WATER

In the loft, reconstructed by Laura Bohn in Manhattan's Chelsea district, all the nuances and tones found in the color of water run along the walls and furniture. From soft green to deep azure to dark smoky gray, nature coexists with the industrial atmosphere in this 19th century workshop.
In the space, open and flooded with light, the decor is reduced to essentials. The apartment is organized into separate functional zones, without walls or space dividers; only the arrangement of the furniture imposes order on the different zones. In front of a comfortable couch covered with taffeta cushions, there is a low white plastic laminate table and two small black tubed easy chairs.
Soft, warm, natural elements alternate with severe, dry industrial shapes; on the gray-blue carpet that covers the entire floor, trees in tubs slide on rollers to catch the sun, moving about among the designer light fixtures attached to window sills, the adjustable spotlights on the ceiling and the decorated cast iron radiators.
To one side of the living space, a wall of subtle blue-green tones is folded like a sheet of paper in a Japanese game, giving breadth to the loft entrance and opening up the kitchen area. Behind the sharp-cornered, slanting kitchen counter are the household appliances, each in its place, and the kitchen utensils are visible on ordinary racks. A low, curved partition leads to the bathroom whose door is combined with built-in shelves in which the TV set is placed. In a corner of the bathroom there is a huge round metal tub, enamelled in Veronese green. Shielded, but always open to the rest of the house, is a private zone for the bedroom, approached through a full height door opening set at an angle to the line of walls.
Sophistication and simplicity join hands in this house in which color is subordinated, without accent, allowing the smell and taste of nature to emerge.

The living zone and, in the background, the kitchen area are bordered by a plastic laminate counter and a folded partition. The high level of illumination throughout the loft is guaranteed by closely spaced perimeter windows, shielded by pierced vinyl blinds. Soft, warm, natural elements alternate with disciplined industrial shapes.

(Top):
the roof-terrace and fire escape of Laura Bohn's loft. In the background, a detail of the Manhattan skyline with streamlined roof top water towers silhouetted against the sky.

(Below):
entrance to the bath, with its special door. The cold, intense gray of the wall emphasizes the "industrial" background of some of the furnishings.

(Large picture):
the dining corner's furniture is kept to essentials and stands free in the space. Theater-type spotlights are suspended from pipes that run across the ceiling.

(Upper left):
another view of the living room. Potted trees let nature enliven the space. The simplicity of the interior design and the use of a few carefully chosen items of furniture markedly expands the open spaces of the apartment. Nature coexists with the industrial ambiance of the 19th century workshop.

(Lower left):
the kitchen area opens directly onto the living area. All kitchen fixtures and utensils are open to view. The counter virtually separates the two areas.

(Upper right):
view of the bedroom through a full-height opening aligned at an angle to the walls. This allows maximum interpenetration of spaces but at the same time gives required isolation to private areas of the house.

(Bottom right):
the huge, round, metal tub enamelled in Veronese green. Sophistication and simplicity are combined in this house in which color is subordinated.

DESIGNING IN WHITE

"Tender Architecture,"
a creation by Alessandro Mendini in a white, synthetic material

THE RATIONALE OF WHITE

"Precise volumes and unquestioned geometry: the rationalists' houses were white; when something was not white, a railing, a fastening, a hand rail, then it was black. Under a white ship, with three cylindrical smoke stacks outlined against the sky, Le Corbusier was signing his epic caption: 'Architecture is a knowing, rigorous, magnificent play of volumes arranged in light.'"

This definition can well serve to introduce the house that architect Mario Botta has built in Switzerland, near Lugano, calling it "The Round House." The aristocratic tower rises, solitary, in a gentle green plain, as in a great piazza. Its round body, in light gray concrete block, is furrowed by a generous cleft made up of two arms which unite into one as they rise to the roof, allowing glimpses of the row of windows within. At the top, the opening runs along the full diameter of the house, and allows light to drop down to the interior below. Behind, the round shell seems to become lighter, almost rising from the ground, leaning against the imposing, robust tower. Inside, the living room appears withdrawn from the entrance. The soft couch and the white, round-cornered table run the length of the low, rectangular opening of the fireplace. In the middle, a bright, blank entry is punctuated and emphasized by cylindrical white plastered columns. Beyond, a glass and timber storage unit shields the dining area and kitchen counter, lined with tall stainless steel stools.

(Large photograph): view of the living room with white couch and round-cornered table in the foreground. The walls, columns and furnishings, white and stark, seem to thread themselves gently between the warm tones of the exposed concrete of the ceiling and the floor of shining strips of fine wood.

(In the small photographs, from left to right): the cylindrical body of the Round House, marked by deep clefts. The aristocratic house rises solitary from a gentle green plain, as in a great piazza.

(Second picture): back of the house. The round shell seems to become lighter, almost rising from the ground, and resting against the robust, imposing stair tower.

(Third picture): detail of the skylight, extending along the entire diameter of the house.

(Far right): principal facade and entrance. The twin clefts allow glimpses of the continuous strips of windows.

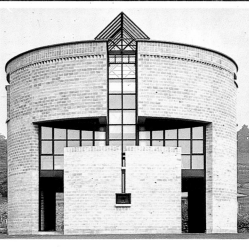

The cleft that cuts the house vertically along its diameter like a spinal column is lit by a long skylight set proudly on the roof, marking out the rooms along its line. On the top floor are the bedrooms and baths.

Inside the round house, the light is taken in and methodically distributed by the governing purity of the white. Walls, columns and furnishings, white and stark, seem to thread themselves gently between the warm tones of exposed concrete of the ceiling and a floor of shining strips of wood.

(Left):
view of the study area, set next to the protruding, circular stairwell. The small space is fitted out with "Tadini" bookshelves and the "Spaghetti chair" by Giandomenico Bellotti.

(Center):
passageway from dining area to living area, lit by light streaming down from above.

(Top left):
view of the skylight with its metal framework, which leads to ground level as a long, full-height window.

(Top right):
the central spine which cuts along the north-south axis of the cylinder of the house, lit by the long skylight which rises above the roofline.

(Bottom):
detail of the stair with graphics strictly disciplined by the modular protective grille.

METAPHYSICAL WHITE

The Danish architect Nils Andersen lives in Copenhagen, a merchants' port, in the attic of an ancient palace, among milk-white walls and furnishings of disturbing perfection. Stiffened by the pervading whiteness of the various spaces, the columns, stairs, and sloping overhanging roof all seem to be as two-dimensional metaphysical bodies, lines and surfaces, harmoniously set out in the scene to recreate, deepen and amplify the silent light of the Arctic night. The wooden floor strips appear to be without substance, imperceptibly disappearing towards the walls, like slender, flexible blades. Only the warm yellow of the artificial lighting creates a feeling of solidity and reality. Just as Giorgio De Chirico created and painted the silent incompatibility between art and reality, so the silent white of this house seems to speak in its memory.

(Below): dining area with Arne Jacobsen's classic chairs in painted wood. The round table top is slate and rests on an Eternit base.

(Above):
three details of the study. Lines and surfaces, solids and voids are harmoniously placed in the space.

(Large photograph): the apartment seen from the entrance steps. In the foregound, a chest of drawers by Mogens Koch concealed by a coat of white paint. In the center, in front of the window in the living area, is the big couch on its wood base.

BASIC WHITE

White walls are handled to form embracing curves in an energetic spatial movement inviting accordian folds. The floor is uniformly finished in large, black slabs of natural slate. Against this background, barely resting on it, are large, colored bookcases, an ironic, three dimensional homage to Piet Mondrian's neoplastic compositions. In a law office in central Milan, decorated by Salvati and Tresoldi, color, drawing strength from the white, extends clear and precise, encroaching.

Each bookcase, while respecting a single design scheme, handles its shelves differently. Red, blue, violet, yellow, azure, green are the basic colors linked in a complementary color scheme. The white, framed, emerges without loss of integrity or strength. It expands in ways most natural to itself: lights, half lights, glints that move and give excitement to the volumes. The vitality of this space deliberately proclaims a concept of basic white, yet one that is gay and serene, far from strictness and intense functionalism.

(This page, top): ceiling as well as floor flow continuously through the whole office, from space to space, without intruding beams. The doorways are always full height.

(Bottom): The walls are painted in a glossy white to increase the incidence of light. The curved divider breaks up the strict geometry and creates a pause in the large space.

(Across page): view of the office in yellow and blue on a white background. The diagonal slash of the wall counterbalances the neoplastic feel of the bookcase.

Different color studies of the library table area. The basic colors are red, blue, violet, yellow, azure and green, linked as complementary colors. Each bookcase, while keeping to the same compositional scheme, has a different arrangement of shelves. This is also true of the arrangement of veneered wood desk tops, laid out to meet demands of the various office areas.

UNIFORM WHITE

Bathed in a sea of white, two very different, apparently incompatible spaces are fused into one long, narrow gallery: in his vacation home on the shores of the North Sea, the Danish architect Claus Bonderup has set his studio and the garage for his vintage, white sports car into one space.

The uniform white gloss on the walls evokes a saline atmosphere, pulling in the feel of the sea, holding and amplifing the resonance of the wood strip floor on which the sports car moves as it enters and leaves. The narrow, separated floor strips of natural pine stop at the solid step of the house, shining and disciplined, unexpectedly set off from the walls to mark the limits of the two spaces. At the far end of the living area, a work table with a white marble top is lit by large glass doors which open onto a sunken terrace.

(Above):
the narrow garage with the sports car's magnificent front. The sea air has given a silver patina to the floor strips of clear pine.

(Right):
the studio area of Claus Bonderup's vacation house. The small terrace, facing south, is protected from the winds by a high embankment. The wall lamps are Claus Bonderup's own design.

THE BRIGHTNESS OF WHITE

In delightful, mannered Paris, architect Jean Satosme has created his home and office out of a 19th century printing shop.

The magic of neon signs is like strands of color suspended in space. Like neon lights, these lines of color against the white of the walls have the magic of flying objects, things suspended in air. Sky blue for the open joists of the old workshop; two tones of green and rose juxtaposed at doors and windows — a cheerful green to the outside, an intimate candy pink to the inside.

The sloping roof is opened up by the large panes of glass of the skylights. In this white house, light is reflected everywhere, moving about freely. Sunlight falling from the skylights meets and mingles with sunshine streaming in at the lower levels. The activities of the house are organized in two levels: office and reception-living are on the ground floor, gathered around a half circle of steps covered, like the rest of the floor, with a white carpet; on the upper level are the dining room, bedrooms and bath/kitchen. The two levels are linked by large, spectacular internal windows.

In the design every part manages to keep its own independent expression, to hold on to its own special space. The technological and urbane modernity of the open joists, trusses and large openings is able to live with the intimate, romantic handling of the soft surfaces, the door and window frames, and the antique furniture. Color, even when used in disciplined, functional amounts, fails to diminish the festive, friendly result.

(Top):
view of the reception/living area with semi-circular steps in white carpet, and an antique table of clear finished wood. The large French windows, framed in green, open to an inner courtyard.

(Bottom):
the bath is directly adjacent to the bedroom. Roof vault and walls are glossy white. The tub, which is reflected in a mirror with a gilded, antique frame, is raised.

(Across page):
the dining room has an openly rationalist feeling. The chairs around the plate glass table are the Cesca by Marcel Breuer.

(Above):
A look from the office through the large window yields another view of the reception/living area on the ground floor. All internal openings (door/window) are in two tones of rose, while doors which open to the outside are in two tones of green.

(Right):
A corner of the dining room shows large plants which are found all over the house. From the large balcony-window an observer can view the office below. The sloping roof is almost all glass, in a complicated framework of open joists and skylight framing.

WHITE AND BLACK

White and black are absolute colors, without nuances and impurities. The one dazzlingly reflects every luminous ray of light and mixes every color; the other greedily absorbs them as it devours and negates light. As opposed symbols of good and evil, light and dark, each of the two colors can, even alone, express antithetical values and signals within our symbolic world. Black can denote distress and sinning but also authority and luxury; white can make us think of innocence and freshness but also of age and wisdom.

In the design and manufacture of furniture and other furnishings of the last decade, the two colors have often been used by assimilating and fusing their characteristics.

The colors white and black, similar and compatible, as covers for couches and lamps, television sets and computers, express the discipline and function of the design intent; indifferently absorbing iron and plastic, glass and leather, promising an ambience of pure technology.

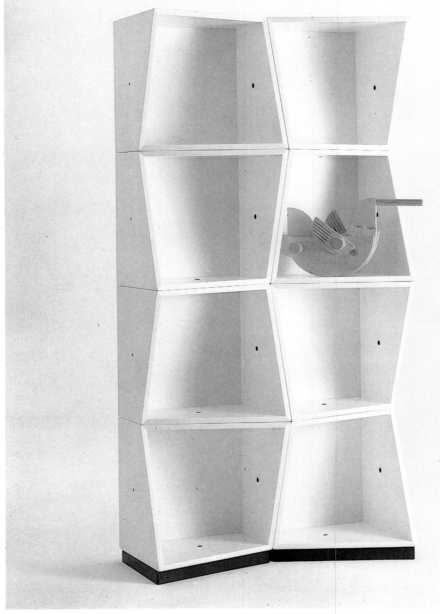

(Top):
Lineare K is furniture assembled from units, some of whose parts are at a 45 degree angle. The units, which are screwed together, may be assembled to form a large variety of overall shapes. The pieces can stand against walls or be used as a space divider, in which case the open faces of units can face in two directions.

(Bottom left):
a child's wooden high chair, with color decorations to the design of Mario Tudor.

(Bottom center):
model in synthetic materials by Vittorio Gregotti. A swimming pool is surrounded by a structure used in a design for the University of Palermo.

(Bottom right):
a photographic study by Antonia Mulas of the classic "Paolina" day-bed, which is again in production.

(Across page):
the long. monumental portico surrounding Aldo Rossi's house in the Gallarate district of Milan has an unusual display of recent white furniture designs.

COLOR AND TECHNOLOGY

Railroad station at Zurich Airport, designed by
Schim, Leber and Walter.

RED ENERGY

With the longest wavelength and the least amount of expressed energy, red is the warmest color, one that can move fastest and still remain visible. It is always the first color to be perceived and recognized. Red is the color of life, of passion; it is the color of vice, of excess and energy.

Martin Wagner belongs to the technological generation of architects. The house which he has built in Hofstetten, Switzerland is a perfect, complex and showy mechanism for producing and using thermal energy and to recover and transfer heat. Solar panels, piping, equipment and machinery are clearly exposed, underscored and unified by the red color of the window and door frames and of the beams — the only artificial color to be used in this machine-like house. Concrete, iron, glass and aluminum take on the warmth and vitality of red; the house rises confidently out of the landscape, an eloquent example of solar construction.

The rectangular prism of the house lies along a north-south axis; with the all-glass, main facade designed as a passive sun collector facing south.

(Above):
exterior of the solar house. On the second floor, there is a balcony with a protective parapet, pierced by two stacks from the fireplace below. Two concrete columns flank the balcony and support the sharply jutting cornice.

(Below):
detail of the glass facade. The glass is insulating and reflective, and on the inside it may be shielded by folding Persian blinds. Frames and spandrels are steel, finished in red baked enamel.

(Across page):
second floor view shows the opening to the battery of solar panels. The mechanical system is used as a meaningful graphic color element.

(Top):
the principal facade,
facing south. On the right
is the separate garage
structure. An impression
of the complex emerges
from the exposed
concrete parapet coping.
On the roof, the battery of
solar heat panels is
visible.

(Below):
the north facade. The
ground level has been
raised using material
excavated during
construction, creating a
place for burying heat
pump components.

In the middle of the facade, a balcony juts out, bordered by a metal-faced parapet and perforated by striated ducts from the fireplace below. On the opposite facade, the semicircular glass block stair tower projects, flanked by metal air ducts. Here, as on the sides, openings are kept to a minimum, and the exposed cavity concrete block walls provide the main visual expression.

On the roof a battery of solar collector panels and the heating plant are covered by metal siding, from which the two air ducts emerge and run exposed. The solar heating installation pumps warm water that feeds directly into the distribution network. When there is insufficient direct sun, a heat pump switches on. Buried on the north side of the house, it uses ground heat, and needs only a small amount of electricity. The active part of the system is integrated with the passive; it is characterized among other elements by a roof pool which reflects the sun's rays to the collectors and which acts by night as a protective filter for inside rooms, avoiding sharp temperature changes. The strictly rational interior is marked by light wells and red baked enamel hardware, by artificial lighting equipment and by the warm brown of the tile floor.

(Top):
view of the north side of the building shows detail of the semi-cylindrical stair well, enclosed in glass.

(Center):
view of the central room on the second floor, opening onto the balcony and showing the two metal ducts and parapet wall.

(Bottom):
stair to the upper floor runs inside the semi-cylindrical glass block wall.

59

TECH-APPEAL

The glass cage is articulated by slender iron columns. The metal curtain wall is carved out with large, clear openings. Strong colors and pastel tones mark the structure and services. This house, built in the Hollywood hills by architect Peter de Bretteville, is a clear example of 'tech appeal,' a design concept that redesigns living space using technology and materials taken over from an industrial tradition. The inside, which is almost all visible from outside, hinges in the middle on a service spine, kitchen and bathrooms. The spine extends to the roof. This large column, in white, separates the house into two generous, two-story areas: living space and office space. The bedrooms on the second level are supported by big, egg-yellow I-beams. A walkway with an open grille flooring runs the length of the house, suspended from cantilevered brackets and flanked on one side with long bookshelves. A pink steel stair with pipe and wire railings extends down from the second level. The busy framework of open joists which supports the roof is painted blue. Color is distributed carefully throughout the transparent space, helping the eye unravel the network of open joists and distinguish one element from another. It does not indulge in rhetorical flourishes to glorify the engineering values of the building, but stays politely in the background.

(Right):
living space. The steel stair links day-time with night-time areas. At the top to the right, a walkway runs the length of the house, above the library.

(Small photograph):
south facade of the
building designed by
Peter de Bretteville. The
facade, which faces the
valley, has more than 350
sq. ft. of glazing.

(Right):
a flight of stairs connects
the two levels. The skin is
sheet metal, supported by
a framework painted
white, a color used for all
other structural elements.
Only the large I-beams
are in egg-yellow.

(Far right):
the walkway that runs
above the living area is
lined with bookshelves.
The web members of the
open web joists are
painted a metallic sky
blue.

ELECTRIC BLUE

Blue is the color of serenity and of royalty. It is the color of the spirit and the infinite, but also of work and of mechanical things: sea and sky, blue overalls and laser beams. The architect Ennio Chiggio has rebuilt an abandoned machine workshop, creating his own design office and an atelier for weaving. The door recalls ship and airplane doors; columns are intentionally and clearly out of proportion; the stair is sturdy and solid. All the mechanical parts of furnishings are painted the colors of industrial electrical installations, with blue dominating along with yellow and black.

On the street side, the patterned metal siding of the walls is strongly expressed, and insulated on the inside with expanded polyurethane sheets. The door is cut into the metal wall as though into a sheet of paper, and is edged by a zinc-plated, yellow-painted rolled steel angle section.

Inside, the space is divided horizontally by the striking blue

(Above):
The door to the studio is patterned in metal sheeting painted blue. The metal siding is insulated internally with expanded polyurethane sheets. The door is cut into the metal siding and is edged with zinc-coated, yellow painted angle irons.

(Right):
Ground floor of the studio-atelier. The walls are white-washed. The stair, painted in the colors of electrical power plants, leads to the attic.

underside of the attic. On the ground floor is the design studio; above is the atelier for weaving. The walls are whitewashed and the tile floor is also a pure, shining white tile. The pit formerly used for motor maintenance contains a stair and is used as a warm air heating plant. The big, round attic beams become thinner as they are bolted to the column heads. Below are the storage units and the large drawing boards and, leaning against the walls like a relic, the classic Rietveld Red and Blue chair. On the left, opposite the stair, bookshelves run the length of the wall.

Above in the attic, the fir floor is black, finished with a shiny, dense, marine varnish. The roof, finished with wood boarding, includes two skylights. The yellows and blacks of the few metal furnishings fade before the riveting authority of the loom and the play of colored wools.

With its bolts and washers, sheet plate and connections, color and materials, the massive iron architecture of this electric blue interior seems to cry out to preserve the spirit fo the old machine shop, but without nostalgia or mummification.

(Top left):
the entrance, with one of the iron columns supporting the attic floor. Against the wall is Rietveld's Red and Blue chair.

(Below):
the motor service pit, fitted with a stair; it now houses the warm air heating plant.

(Across page, top):
this floor is used as a design studio, furnished entirely with colored metal furniture. In the background, bookshelves cover the entire wall.

(Across page, bottom):
view of the attic used for weaving. To light the space, two skylights have been cut into the roof. The floor is black varnished fir.

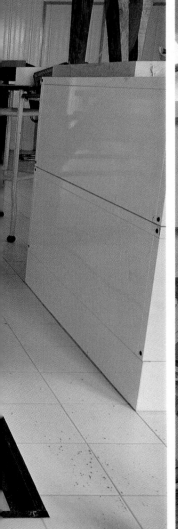

HIGH-TECH COLOR

The metallic glint of hot air ducts, the sinuous black shape of the perforated-sheet stair balustrade, express distinctly the high-tech flavor of this apartment. The architects, Enrica Invernizzi and Sergio Crotti, have set out to reconstruct this house, in an ancient palace, leaving the wall structure untouched.

The warm air heating system uses exposed suspended ducts which weave along the soffit of the ceiling, barely grazing the walls. Even the bathroom is suspended, fastened to a large truss and resting against the glass block wall which lights it. The heavy sheet metal of the stair rail, with its regular pattern of circular perforations, is normally used in the manufacture of industrial filters. Services, piping, electrical wiring and outlets are not camouflaged but highlighted in color. Common industrial products are used for which new uses and new purposes are invented. Both these design concepts commonly defined as "high-tech," are found here, controlled and assimilated.

The silvery shading of metal, the gaudy shine of baked enamel, the infinite color tones of plastic and resins hint at spatial relationships, creating unexpected volumes and new highlights in this high-tech house.

Living room, with couch covered in blue velvet. In the background, the big yellow domestic boiler has exposed ducts emerging from it. On the right, the black dividing wall is not full height, to avoid contact with the structure.

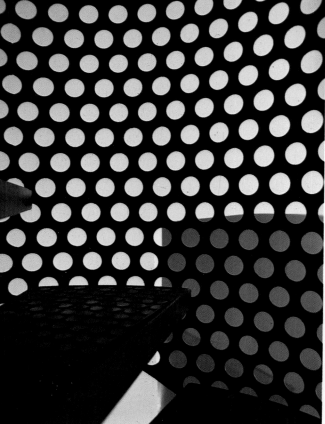

(Across page):
the sinuous shape of the stair that leads to the bedroom. Steps are finished in black, anti-slip rubber with a round profile.

(Above):
the large glass wall of the bathroom. The wash basin top is finished with red tiles.

(Bottom left):
the pierced sheeting of the balustrade and a detail of the steps, finished in industrial rubber flooring.

(Bottom right):
the bathroom is suspended from the large truss, and does not touch the original wall structure.

PAST AND PRESENT

The little old pink house still stands out, with its restful pitched roof; slightly below it, sturdy and oblique, new construction enfolds it, green, black, unexpected.
Frank Gehry lived in a small traditional house in Santa Monica, California. After he decided to enlarge it, he designed an envelope of irregular, surprising volumes: the small pink house was left intact, but its doors and windows became internal openings – links between the new and the old. Yet the two structures did not lose identity, which remains distinct and unmistakable because of color and shape.
The highly personal language of Gehry composes in wood a closely spaced and rhythmical pattern of beams and columns, unexpectedly torn by sharp, explosive windows and skylights that light up and warm the living room, kitchen and dining room. Traditional American construction is used in a masterly way to achieve new and unexpected results.
Outside the area of the old house, the asphalt floor of the dining room and kitchen suggests the sensation of being still outdoors, in the street.

(Above):
outside view of the Gehry house, with the old pink house framed by the new green and black addition.

(Right):
the dining area in the new part of the house is lit by large openings which break up the walls with surprising forms and rhythms.

Green canvas chairs around the metal leg, garden-type table help to make the space hesitate, hovering between feelings of indoors and outdoors. Large trees which surround the house enter through roof openings and give a suffused green light to the walls. The kitchen is a long, narrow glass room, companion to the sea green color of the movable storage units and the white wood framed, glass-covered storage cabinets.

The ceiling, with its slender framing, is crossed by an electric wire cable connecting the small, white, porcelain lamps. In the living room, the wood floor is skillfully used as the basic design element, hollowed out to form a couch area or rising to create partitions or table tops.

(Top):
upper level roof terrace, with one corner pierced by an irregular skylight over the kitchen below.

(Center):
view of the dining area from the living room window opening.

(Right):
the U-shaped couch with its wood framework.

(Top, across page):
the kitchen is conceived as a glass gallery; it has an asphalt floor.

(Bottom, across page):
the breakfast area (at left) includes a work by Chuck Arnoldi on the wall; to the right, another view of the kitchen.

NEW-USES

The high-tech object comes into our home freed of its original function, and welcome as something to be put to a variety of uses. The supermarket shopping cart becomes a magazine rack, pipework is transformed into a chair, a dolly into a tea cart.

Usually this has happened spontaneously, but nowadays industry does it too, stretching the use of certain objects beyond their normal, technical uses. Thus, a lamp may appear under the guise of a hot water heater, or the classic, open web framing of a hangar becomes a support system for theater-type lighting.

Color underscores this change, freeing the object almost entirely from its original use and plugging it into our domestic world.

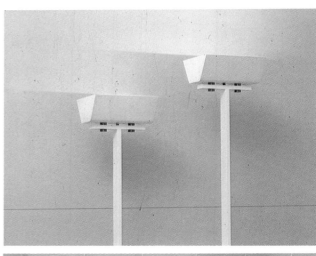

(This page): inside of a prefabricated house, with selected furnishings. Artifacts and furniture are all mass-produced items. Today, even industry has acquired a taste for a new look at high-tech objects, stretching to the limit the applications of certain products. Strong use of color reinforced this tendency.

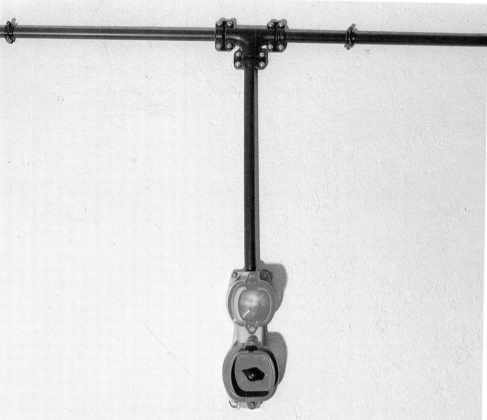

(Left-hand column, from top to bottom):
a self-supporting lighting system on mass-produced open joists; nesting trays of a light alloy; a counter on wheels, in enamelled metal; a movable supermarket shopping cart.

(Right-hand column, from top to bottom):
detail of a colored high-tech artifact; a movable tool-chest in red and blue enamel; detail of the Raccordo design by architect Angelo Cortesi, in which standard pipe and pipe fittings make up tables, chairs and armchairs.

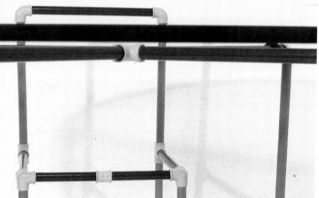

NEW DIRECTIONS

Detail of a corridor in a space designed by
architect Michael Graves

THE HOUSE AS THEATER

Arches, columns and cupolas, stairs, spring boards and deck chairs — the illusory and the theatrical, design and makebelieve, suggest a new dimension to living space. The house is no longer a repository of memories, an intimate, protected space; it is transformed into a space that is imperfect, inconclusive, open to adventure; it stimulates action and gives rise to feelings, not memories; it asks for actors and spectators, not residents.

In the living room of this Long Island house, furnished by the French architect Jean-Pierre Heim and with frescoes by him, the painted brick fireplace is framed by two windows through which one sees a real garden, onto which is superimposed the image of the great wall with its paintings. Heim, some of whose other frescoes are also illustrated in this book, says: "I don't want to play with space, using subterfuge suggested by tromp l'oeil; rather I want to respect it. The reality in which we live and work is too serious and suffocating to be considered in only one sense. Within us there exists a dynamic space which should not be compressed, and which imagination can expand and the intellect visualize."

(Across page, left):
a panel in Heim's studio;
the theme of perspective
depth is a constant
source of invention for
creating architectonic
illusion.

(Across page, right):
another panel from
Heim's studio. It
represents a colonnade,
redesigned from a 17th
century engraving by Jan
de Vries.

(Left):
perspective study of
various stairs, carried out
by Heim in a French
doctor's apartment.

(Above):
in the living-room of the
Long Island house, the
painted, brick fireplace is
framed between two
windows through which
one sees a real garden
on which the image of the
great wall with its
paintings is
superimposed.

THE PAPER HOUSE

Jim McWilliam was art director of a Massachusetts paper mill; he now lives in this small Manhattan apartment on the Hudson River. A passionate and devout gardener, McWilliam decorates, refreshes and renews his house, allowing cascades of colored paper to flower. He transplants, takes up, grafts, sows, weeds: the house is filled, takes on color. Paper is easy to work with yet allows infinite scope. The decoration is never finished, it is always on the move, in transformation.

On the walls there are sometimes vari-colored, tangled skeins, shooting stars that seem to be roots or interlaced leaves of tropical vegetation; sometimes, in a large cylindrical vase, soft violet petals flower. One day the floor is gaily sown with confetti-like corianders, small and ungatherable squares of multi-colored paper; the next day, green, blue and red leaves of paper are placed in high piles, covered with a sheet of glass, creating improbable but functional tables.

The paper withers quickly and the merry procedure is repeated: the house changes its looks, its atmosphere, its color. The chairs of various types are always there, unmoved, but accomplices to the festivities — the tubular steel casually covered in leather, the welcoming wicker, the imitation, shell-like pink rocking chair, the aristocratic stools with their imitation marble seat.

A play house, simple yet personal, as easy to change as a suit of clothes.

(Top):
in Jim McWilliam's New York living room, a cylindrical shaft with draped flowers is set in stiff folds against a background of multicolored polychrome paper vegetation.

(Bottom):
the skein of roots and filaments is a tangle, a three-dimensional sculpture or carnival-like packaging.

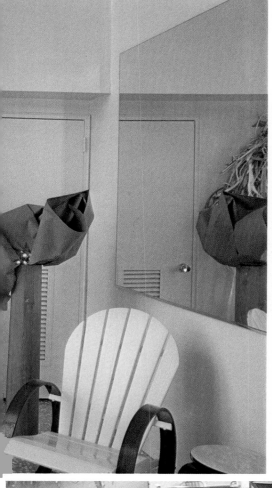

(Bottom center):
paper furnishings as a
balance to the
decoration.

(Top right):
stools with imitation
marble seats. The interest
in paper discloses a
feeling of festivity, of
chaos, of the ephemeral,
even of a dust cloud in
those minute fragments of
color scattered
everywhere.

(Bottom right):
the vase of confetti-like
corianders resembles a
jar of candy. A pink,
imitation shell rocker sits
on a decorative floor.

THE ELECTRIC HOUSE

Color is everywhere, always switched on; neon tubes, halogen lamp fixtures sit immobile on their shafts: the colored lights of a big city at night have come into Charles Swerz and Jerry Van Deelen's New York loft. The house lights up like a big luminous Times Square sign. Private space is indistinguishable from public space; the urban scene comes in through the workshop's big, bare windows, windows without shades or other screening. Lights from street lamps and the big billboards paint intermittent streaks across the walls and ceiling. The bare walls are gray, finished with stucco and plaster of Paris in the same color. On the ceiling, beams criss-cross, dressed in slightly textured plaster. The vast space seems uncluttered and tidy, barely marked by a few, small, still objects. On entering, one is immediately welcomed by the sound and picture of the TV set, which stands like a computerized butler, stiff and impassive, in front of the entrance door, resting on a column pedestal between two windows.

The plaster columns, three feet high and used as shelves, are spread throughout the house, marking time as one moves from one part of the house to another, from one functional group to another: from bed to living-room, from entrance to kitchen. They are ironic archaeological exhibits on this reflected urban scene.

In the center of the loft, four broadcloth covered armchairs are placed around a table in an orderly and strict composition, as if waiting for someone.

On the right, the soft gray carpet rises and curves to protect an alcove, the only private, intimate, almost hidden space in the house: the big bed with its soft mattress and spring. On the left, the sharp rising curve of the partition that separates the kitchen allows a view of the refrigerator, cooking stove, electrical appiances and the large white shelf under its halo of blue neon. In the background, just beyond Samson, the large, five legged table

designed by Gaetano Pesce, there are, gathered in a narrow passage, the lounge and study areas, the most relaxed and lived in part of the house. A friend, speaking of the loft colored in pink, yellow, red and blue lights, said: "The house, when it is empty, is a festival, an art gallery, a self-portrait to come back to at night for a short break while waiting for people to arrive."

(Across page, top):
the bedroom area, with its curve of carpet.

(Across page, bottom):
to the left, the study; to the right, the wall curve that encloses the kitchen space.

(Above):
top photograph shows living area.

(Bottom):
the wall facing the entrance. Recalling the Pop Artists of the 60's, who always had television turned on in their rooms, the column pedestal sets the character of the house as it welcomes guests.

HOME OF THE ARTIST

The walls of our house are like blank pages, open and inviting, on which we can trace a pictorial diary of our feelings, our wishes and our memories. The desire of New York's subway artists to express themselves spontaneously through symbols and color has infected us, and our rooms are being filled with multi-colored decorations, frescoes, as though they were pictures from our autobiography. It remains a private, individual action, but the trend is widespread and significant. The house of Emilio Tadini, shown on these two pages, is only a pretext to talk about the trends and to reflect on them. The artist looks at the walls in his house as canvases, endless opportunities for painting pictures. The house comes alive with pictured puppets, with deeply disturbing sensations, with abstract geometrical decorations.

Perhaps artists have always given concrete shape to the spaces they live in, to the images of their fantasy world. Now they can teach us to do so too.

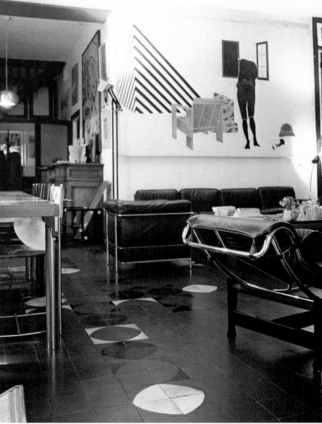

(Top):
view of the studio of painter Emilio Tadini, lit by a skylight.

(Middle):
corner of the room into which are crowded objects and furniture which the artist has placed about with great freedom. In the foreground is Le Corbusier's chaise longue and behind it Rietveld's Crate 1 chair.

(Bottom left):
view of the apartment from the terrace. The French window frames one of the artist's famous canvases.

(Across page):
the low screen with its
three decorated panels.
The screen transforms
itself, giving life to three
fantastic puppets: the
farmer, the old lady and
the jazz trumpeter.

(Above):
a high screen divides the
living area into two
distinct spaces. Even
these surfaces have been
used by the artist for a
composition of cubist
inspiration.

DESIGNS IN COLOR

In the manufacture of furniture and articles of furnishing, industry has clearly gone beyond the "natural" phase of the 70's: clear finished wood, undyed fabrics, plain metal. New, colored surfaces dominate: laminates, baked enamelled metal, painted wood, molded glass and colored fabrics.

The cultural and commercial influences of post modern architecture have shifted the boundaries in the field of industrial design as well. Along with occasional rigid applications of stylistic cosmetics, a general (though not uniform tendency) has developed which makes use of the liberation of forms to conceive or discover new types of products and new functional relationships. A trend has emerged to redesign our domestic world, sometimes fanciful, sometimes refined. These are experiments that perhaps find their best roots in the history of radical and provocative design, in search of an almost ironic theatrical quality in the house of the future.

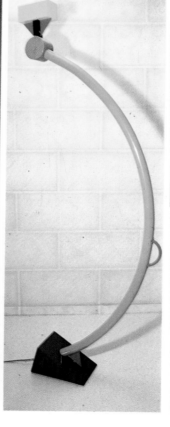

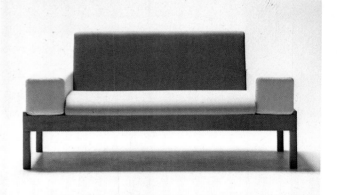

(Across page, top): adjustable easy chair designed by Toshiyuki Kita. The removable cover can be of various colored fabrics.

(Middle): Gibigiana table lamp by Achille Castiglioni. The structure is aluminum in various baked enamel colors.

(Across page, bottom): designed by Gaetano Pesce, this is one of the best and most provocative examples of radical design tipical of much advanced contemporary effort.

(Top, left): the Squash armchair by Paolo Deganello, with the high, enveloping backrest and base in contrasting colors.

(Top right): the Carlton divider, designed by Ettore Sottsass.

(Bottom, left): "Plutone" halogen light fixture, in white opal glass with blue crystal base, designed by Daniela Puppa.

(Bottom center): another design by Ettore Sottsass, a colored, free-form floor lamp.

(Middle, right): the Dafne series of folding chairs, designed by Gastone Rinaldi.

(Below): in the Demel couch designed by Sottsass Associates, the gray of the base and back rests plays games with the different colors of arm rests and seats.

THE COLOR OF PRECIOUS MATERIAL

To design with prudence, silently, letting the materials themselves take an active part, and express themselves by juxtaposition, colorful games, small liberties and contrast--that is one of the strongest current directions. It is based on renewed use of the precious materials of traditional construction, combined with use of refined and sophisticated techniques.

Taken on a summer's day in the hills near Vicenza is this view of the ground floor of this 19th century villa, reconstructed and furnished by architects Flavio Albanese and Maria Luisa Tuorto Meneguzzo.

There are slabs of stone on the floor, blue-tinted walls, a few pieces of furniture placed so as to gather and concentrate the colors of the reflections, the bright nuances of the space.

(Small picture): over the columns, masked by two beams finished in plaster, are two structural steel members, painted in counterpoint to the walls. The floor is Lara stone inlaid with Carsian stone.

(Large picture): view along transverse axis of the house shows light touches of color on the legs of the new model Canova couch, by Flavio Albanese. Aggregato light fittings designed by Enzo Mari extend out from the walls.

(Across page):
walls are finished in plaster tinted with blue oxide. Armchair is from the Genova series. On the wall to the right are Quarto light fixtures designed by Tobia Scarpa.

(Above):
view of the livingroom. The fireplace wall, finished in a fine violet, stands out from the mirrored wall.

(Left):
framed by massive columns is a view of the house and furniture arrangement, with the window looking out over the fields. The table, of iron sections and with a Cugino crystal top, and the Sof-Sof chairs painted in sky blue, were designed by Enzo Mari.

A GRAPHIC LAYOUT

The frames circumscribe, providing a sense of limit and clarity to sudden movements of bright yellow or light colored blue. They attain a three dimensional character, pulling together the random colors of book jackets and household articles.
It is difficult to use color in interior design, to control it and manage its impact and outbursts. The decorative discipline of this space carried out by architects Salvati and Tresoldi was done with special attention to the phenomena of visual perception and to a highly controlled use of graphics. The result is a chromatic harmony that moves along in a precise way from living room to bedroom. Within the regular geometry of this interior, carried out over an existing fixed structure, the large, soft Wink armchairs by Toshiyuki Kita may be moved around freely, as if they were large, irreverent, undisciplined puppets.

The six small photographs along the top show various examples of fixed furnishings in the Oikos system: open shelving, closets with sliding doors, wardrobes with drawers, storage space with movable doors.

(Middle):
entrance to the bedroom. On the wall, a large, oval mirror by Man Ray.

(Below):
bed is framed by the light blue structure of the niche with open shelves.

(Across page):
view of living-room with the Wink armchairs by the Japanese designer Kita in the foreground. The large space is divided in two by the lightly decorated frame of a partition. The two perfectly symmetrical tables add to the formality, order and rigorous geometry of the space.